HOW TO STOP SUICIDE

AND

SUICIDAL THOUGHTS

AND

LIVE A NORMAL LIFE AGAIN

ANGELO O. ONEKA

TABLE OF CONTENTS

CHAPTER   **PAGE**

CHAPTER I

GOD'S PURPOSE IN YOUR LIFE

OUR LIVES

No one knows God's purpose in our lives, and how He works is a complete mystery. Sometimes things can get so bad that we feel that we are totally done, yet God's purpose may just be beginning to unfold in our lives. At times, when things get so rough and the going gets so difficult, those may just be the beginning of new a chapter in your life. They may be announcing the arrivals of good things in your life. Do not let the tough time throw you off board, because your days are just beginning. New chapter of your life is unfolding. Be strong and hang on for your great days are just beginning to emerge.

HELL

You may be thinking that by committing suicide, you may end your troubles or sufferings, but you are absolutely wrong. Your troubles are just beginning where you are heading now. Remember, by committing suicide, you will contravene God's Law or commandment of thou shall not kill. If you do that, you will be guilty of killing yourself, and you will be thrown straight into hell where your sufferings will be enormous and endless. Do you really like that? Is that where you want to go? Are those sufferings and torments the ones you are looking for? Do not make that costly mistake. Your earthly troubles can end, all what you need to do, is to work on them, and surely you will overcome.

TO GOD ONE DAY IS LIKE A THOUSAND YEARS AND ONE THOUSAND YEARS IS LIKE ONE DAY

God's time is totally different from ours. For us waiting for something to happen for example in a five years period, is like nothing is at all is going to happen, and is like waiting forever. With each day that passes, more doubts build up in our minds. And by five years, all the dreams are dead and buried. There is completely no trace of any dream, but to God, those five years are nothing.

For God, one day is enough to create another world. Waiting for a thousand years is like waiting for just one day. So do not be anxious for nothing because things are not happening, they way you want them to happen. Be patient, do not rush. There is no need to rush, let everything in your life take their courses. And what will you gain by committing suicide? Nothing, but you be known as a coward and a loser. Besides, you will be discredited by people, however much you might have achieved in life. Suicide is for cowards and weak-minded people.

OUR EYES

Our eyes are completely blind when it comes to the seeing into the future. Though we can see the physicals in front of us and far off, yet when it comes to the future, we can not even see beyond second. And since we can not see into the future, why then do you want to commit suicide when you do not know what is coming your way in one second? You could commit suicide now and yet your blessing is deemed to come in two minutes. What sense is that? We all go down the valley at one time or the other and we also come up the hill in an unexpected way and sometimes instantly. We virtually control nothing in this world. We claim to, but in reality we do not. Things most of the times happened in accordance to the set time, in other words they are pre-destined. Sometimes we heap ourselves with praises for what has happened to us, saying they all happened because of our own efforts, yet some of them may have happened mysteriously, well beyond our comprehension. Since we do not see into the future and do not control most of the events, it becomes totally pointless and hypocritical for you to think of committing suicide. You are better off leaving your troubles to your creator than trying to take your life. Be patient and wait for God's blessings in your life. They will surely come but at their set times.

CHAPTER II

YOU DO NOT KNOW WHERE YOU ARE GOING

Death is like tomorrow. No body knows what is in tomorrow. It could bring good things and it could also bring bad things.

Death too is a complete mystery. When one dies, one is not sure of where one is going. It is a complete concealed darkness. You could die for worse or for good. Know one knows. So do not be pumped up that you are putting your problems to rest. Not year my dear. Yes, you may escape the earthly troubles but you are not sure of what problems await you where you are heading. The troubles that you are going to face there are hidden from you. The troubles you may face there may be ten times or even more, than the ones you are facing right now. The worst thing with it again, is that you will not be able to escape them like you are able to escape the earthly problems. If you land in troubles there, you will not be given a second chance to come back to this world, so that means, you will be stack in your problems with absolutely no chance to escape.

FACE THE PROBLEM HEADON

However huge and complicated your problem may be, let me tell you that every problem has a solution. So do not be trouble because of its hugeness and its complexity, but find the right solution to it. I promise you, you will find one. One of the ways to find the solutions to your problem is by asking people about their views of the solutions to this problem you are facing now. I am pretty sure you will come up with more than a dozen solutions. And one of these must work. Another step is by coming with a list of solutions that you might think of. Again, one of these must work. So do not give up so easily because the problem looks totally insurmountable. No, it can be overcome however huge it may be. Nothing in life is unconquerable.

DO NOT BE A COWARD

By trying to commit suicide, you are literally a coward, because cowards normally run away whenever they are faced with problems, but tough people stand firm against any problem and most of the time win.

Do not be a coward by trying to end your life because of the problem or problems you are facing now. However complex and how huge it may be, stand firm and face it with courage. If others have overcome before, what makes you believe that you won't? No, you can also overcome this. Remember, nothing is forever. Everything has an end. And no problem is without solutions. Even you problem can be overcome, has an end and has solutions. Whether you do something about it or you do not, the end time will surely come. However to try to kill yourself is cowardice, hypocritical, foolishness and craziness. Why do you want to kill yourself when you can solve the problem? Remember, thou shall not kill.

GETTING RID OF YOUR PROBLEMS!

If you decide to commit suicide thinking that you are getting rid of your problem, you are dead wrong, because as soon as you commit suicide, you will straight away land into the lake of fire, hell. You may ask me, how do you know that? The answer is in The Bible, that states unequivocally that thou shall not kill. Again you may defend yourself by saying that you have not killed anybody, but wait a minute, you have killed somebody and that somebody is yourself. Did God say, though shall not kill but you can kill yourself? Is that what He said? Though it is your body, yet you have no right to destroy it in the way you think, it is against God's Laws. You have not been given permission by God to do so, and that is why you will be thrown straight in God's prison.

And once there, you will experience the worst eternal problems in your life. I say in your life, because there is life after death. You would wish you did not kill yourself, but it will be too late, and you are not going to be given a second chance.

CHAPTER III

TAKE A GOOD WALK

Having a good walk will help you quite a lot. Apart from providing you with the exercise, it will also provide you with the opportunity to marvel at the wonders of God's creation. You will be able to see quite a lot that will keep your stubborn and betraying brain fully occupied and not betray you anymore. This will also ease those crazy thoughts of suicide from your head.

You will also be able to meet with different people as you walk. These are people from different walks of life. Some of these people, are, well to do people who may be taking a walk, others, may be the middle class. You will also see many poor people, people who are poorer than you. Besides, you may also meet with sick people, and if you want to commit suicide because of your sickness, then you will see these people who are also suffering just like you but are not planning to commit suicide like you are planning.

You will also hear the singing of birds, singing so happily and proudly. These birds have nothing, all what they have are the nests, and what God have given them at the time of creation. Also you will see the wonderful sceneries. Good fresh air will give you real sense of life. And by the time you go back home, you are totally a different person, less tensed than you left for the walk.

WALK AS AN EXERCISE

Walking is considered a form of exercise, and it is. I for one really like to walk. I enjoy it quite a lot. It gives me time to reflect on many things. And when I am totally upset, I normally take walks, and by the time I am back home, I am back with new and clear thoughts. It does me a lot of good. In summer especially, I enjoy a lot of sceneries.

I enjoy looking at the different homes with their beautiful landscapes. Besides, I am fully attracted to the beautiful lawns with nicely cut grass. Also I am more attracted to the beautiful flowers all around, totally amazing. I can walk for hours marveling at the beauties of different homes and the lawns.

Try it and you love it. It will bring back life to you. And by the time you go back home, you have given your body the exercise it needs. The good thing with walking, is that, you rarely get tired, and you always feel good.

WALK FOR THOUGHTS AND DECISIONS

Walking is not only a means of exercise, but it will also help you in many ways as we have seen earlier. One of the advantages of walking is that, it will bring to your brain a lot of positive thoughts. It also helps you to make meaningful decisions. We all have at one time or the other, have to make some decisions. And some of the decisions we make are not at all thoughtful decisions. Some of these decisions we tend to make in a rush or out of disappointments and are not at all healthy. Many of them turn out to be very destructive. However, the decisions that you arrive at when you are having a walk, appear to be very healthy and very positive and problems solving type.

That being the case, I can assure you that by taking a walk, you will arrive at a decision not to commit suicide. This is so because your whole body is really functioning at this time, and the blood circulation is running normally. Your brain too, is functioning at the normal capacity. It is not idle or incapacitated by the lack of activity, and therefore, it can bring good thoughts and thus enables you to make the right decision.

WALKING CAN BRING YOU HAPPINESS

By taking a walk, you will be able to work on many things, including things that you have already forgotten. Walking will bring them back to your brain. One of the things that walking will do to you is to make you happy.

As you walk, and as said earlier, you meet with different people, some who are friendly, some who are sad, some who are unfriendly, some who are happy and some who are troubled, and the list goes on and on. Besides, you will be entertained by the wonderful sceneries. The sceneries that are, so beautiful to look at. You also have the air that is soul consoling. The atmosphere that is totally different from the one inside your accommodation. All these are soul boosting. They do not only make life meaningful but actually bring your life back to you and drive away the thoughts of suicide. You will feel like living again. Life becomes once more what it is supposed to be. What God intended it to be and with visible meaning.

This exercise is a complete lubrication to your body. By the time you go back home, you are no longer the old person but a fully transformed person ready to go on with life. Fully energized by some of these innovative thoughts that creep into your brain during your walk, you may also want to put into action some of these innovative thoughts. However, when you go back home, do not go back to your dangerous cocoon and energy sucking defeated life, but move forward with those positive thoughts.

WALK TO AMEND RELATIONSHIP

In every family there are always problems, one way or the other. There is no family on earth without problems. And there is no perfect family. Problems can always arise from different issues and sometimes beyond our imaginations. They may also come when you least expect them.

If you happen to pick a quarrel with your spouse or partner, and you become somewhat depressed and also suddenly have a suicidal thought, I would tell you that do not rush to fulfill that wicked thought. It will do you no good, look at the problem from the right perspective and also weigh it against your family. Look at the possible consequences on your family before you implement that mad decision. There are a lot of solutions to overcome this wicked thought. One of them is taking a walk.

Take a walk. As you walk, you will begin to ponder over things, and may be you will also arrive at the conclusion that you were the one in the wrong and therefore, would want to talk to your spouse or partner about this, and ask for forgiveness. Or alternatively, your spouse may be in the wrong as you earlier perceived it, but your brain now is asking you to forgive him or her for the wrong he or she did to you.

The fresh air and the good atmosphere you are getting from walking may also be convicting you and telling you not to commit suicide. Tensions in your head will also ease and will be replaced by clear and positive thoughts.

And when you go back home, and find the atmosphere there still unchanged, do not stay or begin to discuss issues. Let the situation calm down first. Take another walk and give time for the bad atmosphere to settle down. And as you are away, may be your spouse is also engulfed into meaningful thoughts that will eventually bring peace and reconciliation in the family. And this time, when you are back from your walk, and sense that the atmosphere has settled down and conducive for discussion, then go ahead and discuss the issue, otherwise wait for the appropriate moment. If you start the discussion at a wrong time, you might re-ignite the issue, and the problem may start again.

CHAPTER IV

LISTEN TO GOOD MUSIC

Music is magic. Music can do a lot of things for a person. It can make you cry, it can make you sad, it can make you happy, and the list goes on and on.

We also learn that long ago some of the prophets used music as a center point for prophesying. As you can see from these few examples, music is very powerful. It can also do a lot for you.

If you feel so sad and have that evil feeling of trying to commit suicide, listen to good music that you like, the music that makes you happy. Listen to it over and over until you feel better.

You do not need to stay in your corner of gloom and become more depressed and feel that life is over for you. No, life is not over for you, it is just another chapter in your life that is beginning to unfold. Be patient with life and with yourself. You do not need to worry because things will be okay again. What you are witnessing now, is the process in life, and it does not affect only you but everybody under the sky. And they are not trying to commit suicide like you are trying to do.

DO NOT LISTEN TO MUSIC THAT MAKES YOU SAD

Although music is very good to give you peace of mind, yet some music can make you really sad. And if you are in a state of confusion and are suicidal, do not listen to such kind of music or else it will make and give you courage to commit suicide. Stay away from such music to safe yourself from dying.

SOME MUSIC MAY DRIVE AWAY THE DEMON THAT IS TELLING YOU TO COMMIT SUICIDE

Like I said earlier, some prophets used music for prophesies. Music can do quite a lot in one's life. Some of the music may drive away the demon that is encouraging you to commit suicide. And if you have noticed such one kind of music, then keep listening to that one whenever you feel that you are under attack by the evil forces. It will not only give you peace but will also preserve your life.

MUSIC THAT INVITES EVIL SPIRITS IN YOUR LIFE

There are also demonic music that can immediately invite evil spirits in your life. Stay away from such kind of music, in order to avoid worse problems in your life. However, if you decide to go ahead and continue to listen to such music, you will then attract a lot of evil spirits in your life, and the chance of you committing suicide will be more real than before.

CHAPTER V

IT IS A SIN

It is a sin to commit suicide. The commandment of God states quite clearly that thou shall not kill. Committing suicide is a form of killing. It is not killing other people but killing yourself, which I think, is even more serious. That clearly signifies that you are more dangerous than one can imagine, because if you can imagine of killing yourself, the very you that you live for and possibly love, then what are the lives of other people to you!

From that corner of reasoning, that therefore means, you can just kill other people just like you are killing the flies. If you can not have pity on yourself, who will you have pity on?

GOD'S PUNISHMENT FOR YOU

God will surely punish you for the step you may take to kill yourself. If you can punish yourself, what makes you think that God will not punish you? You hate yourself so therefore God should not have pity on you when you commit suicide. For what, when you consider yourself worthless? No one cares about any worthless thing. You have deemed yourself worthless and indeed you have become worthless by thinking of committing suicide. You have also made yourself become a devil hence also the enemy of God, because one who disregards the Laws of God is not worth the mercies of God. What is so serious, so terrible that makes you want to commit suicide? Please do not do it. Although you consider yourself worthless yet to some other people who love you consider you very important and valuable, totally priceless despite what you are currently facing. You are more than gold or diamond to them and God loves you too, so do not commit suicide.

SUICIDE IS MADNESS

It is complete madness for one to think to commit suicide. I know that problems at times are overwhelming especially when you have no where to turn to, but they should not make you to go to the extent of committing suicide. There are always solutions to these very disturbing problems, but we must always look for them. Just as I stated earlier, there is no one single person in this world without problems. Some of these people you see happy and you admire are also in problems but they do not expose them to the public. If you knew their problems, may be you would sleep like a log every night without waking up, because their problems make your problems look like a joke. And if you travel the world and see people's problems, you would want to live forever. You are thinking that you are the only one in serious problems because you do not know the problems other people are facing. Only God has no problems. Some people do not even have a night sleep because of the problems they have. They keep on tossing in the beds the whole nights because problems stop them from falling asleep. Others are in the hospitals and can not even turn themselves. Other people have to turn them. So you think that you have problems? You must be kidding. Go out and see with your naked eyes the reality of life and you will appreciate and thank God for who you are and what you have, but for you to think of committing suicide is a complete madness. Stop it and live your normal life again and be happy despite the problems and good things will come your way. Remember, you have to attract good things. You can not attract good things with your gloomy face and looking like you want to destroy the whole world. In so doing, you are chasing away everything in your life. You quarrel with no one and may be you know no one and yet you look at them with such hate and disgust. In so doing, you are only attracting bad things to yourself, and also making yourself, more depressed, and demonized with the feeling of committing suicide. Stop it and live again.

DEFEAT SUICIDE WITH HAPPINESS

Always stay happy to keep away the evil thoughts of suicide. If your can not stay happy find things that will make you laugh and stay happy. There are plenty of them out there. Some comedies are one of them. Funny and crazy people can also give you the joy of staying happy because they do and say things that are extremely outside the norms of life. Look for these things and never stay gloom and to be tortured by the devil.

CHAPTER VI

VISIT THE HOSPITALS

If you think you are the only one who is in problems, visit the hospitals and see for yourself how people are suffering.

You will see people suffering from different illnesses. Suffering terribly with no hope of getting better or when these sufferings will come to an end. Some of them, will be treated eventually, some may have diseases that are totally incurable, while others will die. Many of these people now can not even turn themselves, they have to be turned by the nurses, many can not dress themselves, they have to be dressed up by other people, many can not walk, they have to be supported by other people in order to walk, while others can not feed themselves, they have to be fed by other people, on and on. Do you think you have problems?

You will totally be surprised and left to wonder why some of these people still choose to live when they are immensely suffering. To your surprise again, these people have not chosen to end their lives like you are trying to do with yours. They want to live despite their sufferings. These are very strong people whose problems would make your problems looks like a kindergarten.

THE WORLD

In the world that we live in, there are a lot of problems, and no one is free from them no matter whoever we may be. Problems also come any time without announcing their arrivals. Besides, they come in different forms. Some are so aggressive and ready to destroy, but we always stand firm against them and we confront them boldly. Some of them, we overcome, others destroy us, while others kill us. However, we must not become cowards by trying to commit suicide. It is not a victory at all by committing suicide.

IN THE HOSPITALS

In the hospitals, you will see people afflicted by different diseases. Some of these people are suffering from heart problems, cancer, hypertension, madness, etc. just to mention but a few. Again, many of these people have not given up on life despite their problems. Remember, some of these people have no hope of living, especially those with incurable diseases, yet they are not thinking of committing suicide. They stay strong everyday and hope that one day they will be cured.

What is your problem that is sending you to commit suicide? Is your problem bigger than their problems? I am sure that your problem is nothing to their terrible problems. Quit that mentality and live a normal life.

Know that everyone has problems of some kind but we are struggling to go on and always hope for the best. If the blessings come, we thank God, alternatively, if they do not come, we just carry on and no need to give up or feel like killing ourselves. It is not the end of the world. You may commit suicide today and yet your blessing was coming the following day. You see how short sighted you are! Do not try it, for you do not know tomorrow. Tomorrow may be your greatest day, never give up, your blessing is on the around the corner. You see, we claim to have eyes and yet we can not even see beyond one second. What have you seen that now tells you to commit suicide? Do you have eyes the kind of eyes that see into tomorrow? Stop it my dear and carry on.

You will one day celebrate that you did not commit suicide. You may become, a great man, you may become the richest man in the world, or may become President of a country. Who knows? Only God knows but we are all blind.

CHAPTER VII

DO NOT STAY ALONE

Staying alone when you are having, suicidal thoughts, is like pulling the grenade pin and holding that grenade in your hand, or dropping it at your feet. It will explode and kill you.

When you have suicidal thoughts and you stay alone, you are merely expediting your suicide, because you get more depressed and more evil thoughts will always invade your clean thoughts.

ALTERNATIVE TO STAYING ALONE

There are so many things you can do to avoid staying alone. You could do any of the following:
1. Occupy yourself with something you like to do.
2. Go to the mall.
3. Go to the library.
4. Stay with your family members.
5. Stay with good friends.
6. Never stay idle.

1. OCCUPY YOURSELF WITH SOMETHING YOU LIKE TO DO

When you are having suicidal thoughts, engage yourself with something you like to do. This will keep you busy and eliminate the suicidal thoughts from your head. Take as long as you can, doing that thing, until you feel there is totally no such thoughts in your head. And if you become bored of one particular hobby or what you are doing, change to another one. The purpose here is to keep you away from the suicidal thoughts.

2. GO TO THE MALL

The malls are places full of activities and things to see. If you are feeling suicidal, these are places you could go to, to take away those toxic thoughts. You have a lot to see and to occupy you. Take your time here until you feel that life has returned back to you. If you have nothing to do, stay there until the closing time, and come back only to sleep. If however, it is too early for you to go to bed, find something to do to occupy you and avoid going back into those deadly thoughts.

You could watch the T.V., any program that appeals to you. Or listen to music, read books, magazines, or newspapers, whatever could occupy you, but do not go home and do nothing, thus, falling into that poisonous thoughts again. This will do you no good, it will only kill you.

3. GO TO THE LIBRARY

Go to the library and get yourself fully engaged. Read books, newspapers, or go online. Do what you like to do and remain fully occupied in order to avoid those suicidal thoughts. If you find something that you really like and that keeps you engaged, go for it. Since you are occupied, you will not know how fast time goes. This is absolutely good for you because it will keep you away from death.

4. STAY WITH YOUR FAMILY MEMBERS

To overcome this evil, stay with your family members. While with them, you will be talking, listening, and possibly laughing too, and you will therefore have no time to be thinking of killing yourself. If you do not have anything to do, keep in this company until you have something else to do, or going to bed. Always try to avoid staying alone and doing nothing, because these thoughts will take on you again.

5. STAY WITH GOOD FRIENDS

Another medicine to avoid having suicidal thoughts, and to avoid suicide, is to have a company of good friends. While with them, engage in talking and listening.

6. NEVER STAY IDLE

When you have suicidal thoughts, never stay idle. By staying idle, the evil thoughts will always dawn on you, and there is a possibility that you may commit suicide because of the overwhelming effects, but when you are fully occupied with doing something, your mind remains in that thing and therefore you will have no time to think.

CHAPTER VIII

SEEK MEDICAL HELP

When you feel suicidal, you should seek immediate medical attention because this is a serious problem. You may not know what you may be suffering from. It could be that you may be suffering from some psychological problems.

These problems need to be diagnosed by the medical doctors. You should not waste time, by wasting time you may find yourself in a coffin very prematurely. Do not do that. Save yourself, go to the doctors immediately and let them help you.

It could be a minor problem or a serious problem such as insanity that is causing you to feel suicidal. Let them diagnose it and treat it accordingly and live a normal life again.

We have also seen that sometimes it could be caused by medication you are currently taking, or lack of sleep and so many other factors, that is why you should immediately seek for the professionals to help you come out of this evil feeling.

MINOR PROBLEM

If it is a minor problem such as lack of sleep or the medication you are taking, the doctors will advise you accordingly, but do not be guessing over this, just by yourself. Minor problem may just be got rid of quickly.

SERIOUS PROBLEM

If however you have a serious psychological problem, such as insanity etc., you will be admitted into the hospital for treatments and observations. It may take a while before you are normal again. The doctors will tell you professionally. However long it may take, that should not be your problem because you want to get well. Don't you? Stay there until they discharge on the grounds that you are now okay.

When you are discharged, you may also be given some medication that you continue to take while you are home. Follow the instructions very strictly, and do not stop taking or skip taking your medication. Finish this medication as prescribed.

And for routine check-ups, you should not skip any of them. Keep on until they tell you that you are now okay. This is for your own good and also to save your life, and may also save the lives of other people, in case you are insane.

CHAPTER IX

YOU ARE NOT ALONE IN PROBLEMS

No one in the world has monopoly over problems. Problems are somewhat equally distributed, although some people seem to have the lion's share. Does it therefore mean that when one has the lion's share of the problems, should one therefore commit suicide? The answer is an absolute no. Why? The reason is crystal clear, nothing, is forever, even problems are not forever. Today, they are here with you and tomorrow, they are with another person. Problems are prostitutes. Therefore do not worry about them. They will surely leave and you will be free again.

KINDS OF PROBLEMS

There are numerous kinds of problems that can afflict one, not once, not twice, and not thrice, but many, many times. Some of these problems are:
1. There are illness problems.
2. There are poverty problems.
3. There are scarcity problems.
4. There are friendship problems.
5. There are family problems.
6. There are children's problems.
7. There are parents' problems.
8. There are work problems.
9. There are school problems.
10. There are driving problems.
11. There are pollution problems.
12. There are smoking problems.
13. There are alcoholism problems.
14. There are drugs problems.

15. There are sleep problems.
16. There are eating problems.
17. There are injustice problems.
18. There are discrimination problems.
19. There are money problems.
20. There are spending problems.
21. There are water problems.
22. There are cooking problems.

And the list goes on and on endlessly, and we are all affected by these problems. No one is free from these problems but we do not resort to committing suicide. Life does not end there, it continues until the right time for us to go comes. We do not invoke this time.

So now you can see that problems are everywhere and they come in different forms and no one is free of them. Now that you know that everyone has problems and not just only you, are you therefore ready to get rid of your mad thoughts of suicide? It is a step in a wrong direction to think of committing suicide. We must always stand firm against problems and look for appropriate solutions outside suicide. Also know that these problems are temporary. They will appear like the wind, so take courage and live on.

CHAPTER X

SOLVE THAT PROBLEM

If your house is on fire, you immediately look for ways to extinguish the fire, and one of the ways is to call fire brigade or firemen as the may be called to come and put out the fire. You would not just stand by and do nothing as the fire burns down your house. That is something totally inconceivable. Anybody would make sure that the house is salvaged. And if you just stand by and watch as fire destroys your house, and you think the fire will have mercy on you and stop burning your house, is a complete boloney. Everyone would definitely make sure that the fire is put out

It is the same thing with problems. If you have problems and you decide to do nothing about them, wrongfully thinking that they will solve themselves, is a total nonsense. Like the owner of a burning house would look for all the means to put out the fire, you too should not rest but look for ways to solve those problems that are disturbing you. Do not expect other people to solve them for you. It is you and it is your absolute responsibility to solve them. Just like the owner of a burning house who stands there and watches his or her house burning and does nothing about it, thinking that the fire will stop by itself, will see his or her house in ashes. You too if problems are all over you and you decide to do nothing about them, you will also see yourself in ashes.

DO SOMETHING ABOUT YOUR PROBLEMS

You can not stand by and allow problems to completely destroy you. You must do something about them. Find ways to solve them. Just like I like to say, every problem has a solution. And we must always look for the right solutions to solve our problems, nor matter what they are, small or huge, complicated or simple.

If you have sickness problem, go to the doctors to get the right treatment.
If you are a drug addict, stop using drug and go for rehabilitation.
If you have the problem of alcoholism, stop drinking too much and go for rehabilitation.
If you have psychosis, go to the psychiatrist for the right treatment.
If like to fight, stop fighting.
If you have become obese moderate your eating habits.
If you are coughing, look for cough mixture.
And the list goes on and on. Solve the problem or those problems that are disturbing you and making you to have suicidal thoughts. Suicide is not a solution, it is a defeat.

CHAPTER XI

MEDICATION

Medication sometimes could be the cause of your suicidal feeling. Some medication can cause quite a number of problems. If you are currently taking some medication, then you need to take a break from that medication to see whether it is the cause of this kind of feeling. Go back to your doctor and explain to him or her how your feeling has changed, since you started taking this medication. May be he or she will realize and write for you an alternative medication.

NEWLY DISCOVERED DRUGS

Newly discovered medicines sometimes can be really a problem. They can be said to work miracles, but after sometime, they may be found to be total health hazard. Many have killed and many can kill. A lot have also been found to have caused serious health problems to those who have taken them. Some of the manufacturers of some of these medicines have been sued, and some are facing law suits even now. Check this with your doctor, if he has prescribed to you a newly introduced drug in the market.

CHAPTER XII

AVOID DRUGS

Drugs are not solutions to any problem, if anything, they are a problem, and are also the means to aggravate problems. When under intoxication of drugs, you may be led to believe that you are solving your problems, or that you have left your problems behind. No, you have not solved your problems nor have you left them behind. Your problems are actually gaining momentum, they are becoming bigger, and bigger day by day and are ready to destroy you. Yet still, you have added one more problem to your current problems that you mistakenly think you are solving. The new problem is drug. This may be the biggest problem now you have, and sure enough, it will destroy you mercilessly. Besides, the authorities will be after you. There are so many problems, drugs can cause you. Some of them are listed below.

PROBLEMS THAT THE DRUGS WILL CAUSE YOU

If you think you are solving your problems by using drugs, look at the problems, drugs will cause you:
1. Imprisonment
2. death
3. Injuries to yourself.
4. Insanity
5. Aggressiveness
6. Murder
7. Injuries to others.
8. Poor health
9. Loss of respect from others.
10. Hatred towards you
11. Cause you to commit suicide

1. IMPRISONMENT

By using drugs, you will be arrested and imprisoned. Is that what you are looking for? It has happened to many, it will happen to you too. It is only a matter of time.

2. DEATH

You can also be killed by your fellow drugs addicts. If not, may be by the law enforcement officials.

3. CAUSE YOU INJURIES

You could end up self-inflicting yourself with injuries or you may be injured by others.

4. INSANITY

Drugs will make you become insane and that is a newly created problem. Do you really like that?

5. AGGRESSIVENESS

Drugs will also cause you to become aggressive towards other people. That also means, you will become anti-social and no one will like you, because you have chosen the wrong path of life.

6. MURDER

Drugs may cause you to kill other people because you have become a half human.

7. INJURIES TO OTHERS

You may also injure other people. This has happened time and again with other drugs users.

8. POOR HEALTH

Besides all these problems, drugs may also cause you poor health. In addition, you will become a vegetable.

9. LOSS OF RESPECT FROM OTHERS

You will never be respected by anybody.

10. HATRED TOWARDS YOU

People will also hate you because of what you are doing, and they consider you a huge problem for the society. And indeed they are right, you have become a huge liability to the society.

11. CAUSE YOU TO COMMIT SUICIDE

Drugs may also cause you to commit suicide because you are insane.

CHAPTER XIII

HAVE ENOUGH SLEEP

Lack of sleep can cause a lot of problems. God made our bodies not to continuously keep on working. He made them also to rest. And night time was made specifically for us to rest. However, in this modern time, some people work at nights, for example, people who work in the hospitals, those who work in the factories, law enforcement officials, etc. And if you work at night, that is a different story altogether, because day time becomes your time of rest. That means, you are going to sleep during day time. No matter what the case, your body needs sleep. Your brain also needs enough sleep for it to function normally.

Lack of sleep can cause a lot of problems as we said earlier. Problems such as:
1. Aggressiveness
2. Weakness in the body
3. Lack of attention
4. It can also interfere with the normal functioning of the brain.
5. Drowsiness
6. Accidents in case you drive
7. Crazy thoughts
8. Lack of concentration.

And the list goes on and on.

CHAPTER XIV

AVOID ALCOHOL

When you are having suicidal thoughts, do not inflame the feeling by taking alcohol. Alcohol may give you the courage you need to commit suicide, so stay away from it. Just be yourself, I mean stay normal.

PEOPLE REACTIONS TO ALCOHOL

People are normally affected differently by alcohol. Some people become very aggressive and always want to fight once they are drunk. They feel that they are the strongest and can beat up everyone. Some people become so happy when they are drunk. Others become so sad and miserable. Yet others are made to cry.

If you happen to be one of those that become so sad and miserable, then do not drink, because drinking will make you commit suicide. Instead of trying to run away fro your problems by resorting to drinking, you should look for viable solutions to your problems. Drinking will not take away your problems but only stupefy you to believe that you do not have any problem, when you really have serious problems. Stay away from alcohol to safe your life, and to get rid of your problems.

CHAPTER XV

AVOID BAD FRIENDS

Having bad friends can cause one numerous problems. Some of these problems can lead to death. It is therefore advisable that one should not associate with such people in order to avoid those many problems. Some of those friends may even cause one to commit suicide. It is not the problems that will cause you to commit suicide, then it will be the bullying of these bad friends. Know that these so called friends are used to doing bad things, and therefore would not mind bullying you. They can even kill you if you disagree with them on some issues.

Let us look at some of the problems these bad friends can cause you. Some of these problems are listed below.

PROBLEMS THAT CAN BE CAUSED BY BAD FRIENDS

These are some of the problems that bad friends can cause you:
1. They can hook you on drugs.
2. The can hook you on smoking.
3. They can hook you on alcohol.
4. They can make you become a thief if they are thieves.
5. They can turn you into a murderer if they are killers.
6. They can injure you.
7. They can even kill you.
8. They can turn you into a vandal.
9. They can turn you into a molester.
10. They can turn you into a bully.

There are always solutions to all problems. Even this has solutions.

SOLUTIONS

1. Do not associate with these bad friends.
2. Re-locate to another place to avoid them.
3. Do not yield to their demand that you use drugs.
4. Stay away from smoking.
5. Reject their violence mentality.
6. Do not get involved in alcohol.
7. Do not become a vandal, etc

These are some of the solutions to the influence of bad friends. Practice them and they will help you to stay away from suicidal thoughts and also from committing suicide.

CHAPTER XVI

GOOD TIME IS AHEAD

If you are having bad time now, know that good time is ahead. Bad time does not last forever. There is an end to everything including the bad time you are facing right now. Your day could be tomorrow, and tomorrow is not very far from now. So why do you want to commit suicide?

Know that everyone has bad time and good time as well, you are not alone, so be strong and you will rejoice in the end. Continue with the fight, the end of the tunnel is not very far away. If you commit suicide now, you are going to miss the blessings God has for you. Do not be in a hurry. Somewhere, they have a proverb that says "The leopard has spotted skin because of the hurry". Its creation was not yet completed but was already hurrying to get away. I do not know for what it was hurrying! And what are you in a hurry for? Stop those suicidal thoughts and do not attempt to commit suicide. You time to die has not yet come, and you do not know when it is coming, it could be a hundred years from now, and it could be even now. Yet when death will be coming to you, you will run away and also cry for help. And strangely enough, now you are thinking of committing suicide.

If everyone was afraid of hard times, and wants to commit suicide, the world would be empty of people, because everyone has problems. Be strong and you will overcome. When hard time is pressing really hard on you, just say to yourself, "even this will pass away and the good time is just ahead of me". And whenever the suicidal thoughts attack you, repeat that saying. Suicide must be defeated and you will defeat it.

CHAPTER XVII

POVERTY

Poverty appears to be one of the major problems facing people today. Many who are suffering from this disease, have lost not only their dignity, but have also become frustrated, depressed, and hopeless. A small number of these people feel that they can run away from this problem by committing suicide. They also wrongly think that by committing suicide their problems are solved but they are dead wrong. Their problems merely resurrect when they commit suicide, because then they will face much worse problems than they are facing right now.

They may go to places where they will encounter with mountain of problems, and the worst thing about it, is that they will not have any solutions to those problems. They will stay in those problems forever. And yet, here on earth, they have left their families in worse states than when they were alive. Both their wives and children will become destitutes. The question then is, if you really love your family, then why do you want to commit suicide and leave your family in terrible problems?

This problem you are facing now is not eternal, it will disappear and leave you alone one day. Why then don't you wait for that day?

Know that there are solutions to all problems. You do not need to commit suicide. Take a look at some of the solutions to your problems.

SOLUTIONS

1. Find a job
2. Go back to school
3. Borrow money and start your business
4. Re-locate
5. Watch your money
6. Get a cheaper place, etc

FIND A JOB

Find a job that will generate for you income. The income that you get will help alleviate some of your problems.

1. GO BACK TO SCHOOL

Go back to school and upgrade your education. You could also possibly take a short professional course that will help you to find a job. By upgrading your education or attending a short professional course, means you will earn more money and thus tackle both poverty and suicidal thoughts ahead on.

2. BORROW MONEY AND START YOUR OWN BUSINESS

Borrow money, from whoever, relatives, friends, institutions if you can, and start your own business and make income not only to fight poverty, but also to put you on the path of financial freedom.

3. RE-LOCATE

May be where you live now is not a good place for you, because there are no opportunities there and does not bring you any blessing. Re-locate to another place where may be you have opportunities to progress and also be blessed.

4. WATCH YOUR MONEY

You could be making a lot of money but if you do not know how to spend your money you will not only be broke, but become poor too. Get away from wasteful spending and put the suicidal thoughts to eternal rest.

5. GET A CHEAPER PLACE

If where you are living now is draining money away from you, making you poor thus making you to have suicidal thoughts, move away from that place. Get a cheaper place that will leave money in your pocket. This step will also help you to get rid of your suicidal thoughts.

CHAPTER XVIII

YOUR SPOUSE OR PARTNER

Is your spouse or partner giving you hard time? Do not worry, the tide will turn, do not give up so easily. I know that some spouses are really horrible, they can be worse than the devil. They can make your life hell on earth. The good news, however, is that there are solutions to every problem. Whatever type of spouse or partner you have now, give him or her time to reform, and go to God in prayers for guidance. Know that you can not change a person, but God can.

You can do everything, however, it may be futile because you are not with this person every time with this person but God watches every time, what we do in darkness and in broad daylight. Secrets are for human beings but to God, there are no secrets. All our secrets are placed right in front of Him. So therefore, leave everything to God.

PRAYER

Pray everyday for the redemption of this person. I know that once a person is living in sins, will always turn away from God and always tries to run away from God. Anything you tell him or her about God or anything to do with God is like an insult to this person. He or she will always resist transformation, but God's powers can never be minimized. He will act at His own time and deal with this person accordingly.

PEOPLE ARE TRANSFORMED

Have you never seen a person who was so bad, but all of a sudden, this person changed into a good person. So do not let the behaviour or the mistreatments of your spouse of partner bother you, let God deal with them, and God will never let you down, I promise you. It is only a matter of time. Do not commit suicide because the great days of joy are ahead of you, and you will be happy that you did not commit suicide. Be strong and love your spouse or partner, despite the mistreatments or bad behaviour, you are currently witnessing.

CHAPTER XIX

YOUR CHILDREN

Are your children driving you crazy? Many parents are normally driven crazy by their children. Children normally do things that their parents do not want them to do. And they also go out and cause problems with other people. When they cause problems with other people, you become the target of their anger and revenge. They will come and vend their anger on you.

LACK OF FOOD

Some parents also may not have enough to feed their children, and as such, there is always chaos in the families. They also get depressed because they are unable to feed their children, or are depressed to see their children suffer. I know it is difficult, but do not let this become a stumbling block for you, or cause you to think of committing suicide. Do you think by committing suicide you are helping the situation? Do not deceive yourself, you are only going to make the situation worse, besides you are going to make your children suffer more when you are gone. What kind of parents are you? Did you bring these children in this world to suffer alone? Think twice before you commit suicide. God is seeing your sufferings and one day He will have mercy on you. Look at some of the celebrities, many grew up in single-parents' homes and suffered quite immensely, but look at where they are today. You too can become like them. Leave your problems to God to handle.

God sees your sufferings and one day He is going to say enough is enough and will reward you very richly. Know that, everything that happens under the sky happens for a purpose. There is no greatness without first suffering. Sufferings are preludes to greatness. Sufferings are also classrooms to learn a lot of things including humility.

Therefore dear, be patient and wait for your great days set before you. You will always thank God for what He has done for you. God is great and He does the impossible. Rejoice and do away with suicidal thoughts, they are of no use to you. They are deceptions and evil, do not listen to them.

CHAPTER XX

YOUR FELLOW STUDENTS

Many students have committed suicides because of bullying from other students. It is however, a wrong thing to bully other fellow students. The authorities everywhere should make bullying a serious offence in order to get rid of this destructive problem.

People send their children to learn and not to be bullied. This kind of crime affects not only the students that is being bullied, but also their parents, the communities, the governments and the countries as well. If allowed to continue, it may cause many students to dropout of schools and that will affect the future manpower, the economy, etc.

WHAT TO DO

There are a number of steps that can be taken to fight bullying. Some of these are:
1. Report the bullying problem to your parents.
2. Report the bullying to the school authorities.
3. Report the bullying to the law enforcement authorities.
4. Change school
5. Stay away from the bullies all the time.
6. Re-locate to another place.

DO NOT COMMIT SUICIDE

Do not make the bullies feel like winners and be proud of what they are doing. Resist any suicidal thoughts. Tell yourself, I do not want them to win, but I must win.

CHAPTER XXI

YOUR CO-WORKERS

Sometimes co-workers can be a thorn in your flesh. They will make your work difficult and at times falsely report you to your boss. There are a lot of things that your fellow workers can do to you. Some of these are:

1. Gossip about you whenever you are away.
2. Falsely report you to your boss.
3. Want your position.
4. Stand in your way if there is a chance for promotion.
5. Pick up problems with you.
6. Steal from you.
7. Despise you.
8. Fight with you.

These are just a few of the long list of what your fellow workers can do to you. However, do not let them get into your skin. You must always find ways how to fight these. Some of these are shown here below.

HOW TO FIGHT BACK

If you are having some problems with your fellow workers, do the following:

1. Make sure you are always early for work in order to avoid being fired as a result of false reports.
2. Do thorough work always, so that your boss will have trust in you, and anyone fighting for your position will always have no room to have it.

3. Do not associate with anyone you know who falsely reports his or her fellow workers.
4. Do not let anyone demean you. Know that you are somebody and always tell yourself that.
5. Whenever anyone of them tries to pick up a fight with you, walk away and let the management know about it so that he or she will be given a warning.
6. Always keep your stuff secured.
7. Always ignore their gossips.

Whatever the problem, do not let them instill in you the thoughts of committing suicide or drive you to commit suicide. If it becomes too much for you, leave that job. You do not want your health to be affected. Do you? Your health is more important, and as for the job, you can always get another one.

CHAPTER XXII

OTHER RELATIVES

Not all the relatives are good relatives, some relatives, are really very bad. They are always there to drag you down and to completely destroy you. They will do everything to make sure that you fail. Remember, these are people close to you and they know your secrets. Some of the secrets you tell them yourself. These relatives want you to live the life below their standard of living. They may drive you to have suicidal thoughts or even commit suicide.

WHAT YOUR RELATIVES CAN DO

As we saw above, your relatives can do a lot damages to you. Some of these malice things are:

1. They may gossip about you.
2. They may destroy your business.
3. They may destroy your marriage.
4. They may lie about you.
5. They may destroy your friendships.
6. If they borrow from you, they may not pay back.
7. They want your husband or your wife.
8. They may want what you have.
9. They may hate you because you are successful.
10. They may even plot to harm you.
11. They may steal from you.
12. They may fight you.

13. They may drive you crazy.
14. They may instill in you suicidal thoughts.
15. They may make you commit suicide.

And the list goes on and on endlessly. However do not give them room to make you commit suicide. Here are some of the steps you can take to defeat their motives:

1. Do not associate with your bad relatives.
2. Do not lend to them.
3. Make sure you securely protect your properties.
4. Do not tell them your secrets.
5. Do not introduce your friends to them.
6. Let your spouse know that they are bad people to avoid problems arising from them.
7. Ignore their gossips.

CHAPTER XXIII

EXAMINATIONS

To pass any examinations, you need to study hard and know your subjects well. If you do not know your subjects well, you will fail. And failing an examination, is, one of the most disappointing thing. It is so time wasting, because you have to study for the same exams again. It will dawn on you for every long time. You will see your peers, progress while you remain stagnant. And if you do not study hard for the repeat exams, you will fail again.

When you fail any examination, it is not only you who will feel the disappointment, but your parents also will be affected. Failing examinations have always caused a lot of problems to the students. We will look at some of these problems herein below:

PROBLEMS ASSOCIATED WITH FAILING EXAMS

These are some of the problems that are associated with failing examinations:

1. Many weak students, who have failed the examinations, have committed suicide.
2. Many have become depressed.
3. Many have dropped out of schools because they think they can not make it
4. Many have resorted to drugs and totally ruined their lives.
5. Many have resorted to alcohol to alleviate their pains, etc

Let me tell you that failing an examination is not the end of life and it does not mean that you are stupid. Just like every problem, has solution, so are the exams. Let us look at some of the solutions to make you pass exams.

SOLUTIONS TO PASSING EXAMS

1. Always study hard.
2. Know your subject thoroughly.
3. Do not party during exams time.
4. Completely avoid drugs, because they will affect the power of your brain.
5. Avoid alcohol especially during exams time.
6. During exams time, put relationships on hold and concentrate in preparations.
7. Avoid those who upset you because the will rob you of your study time.
8. Stay away from cigarette smoke lest it makes you sick, hence you won't concentrate.
9. If you are working, take a leave during this time.
10. On the days of exams, have enough sleep.
11. Do not quarrel during this time or it will affect your preparations.
12. On the exams days, always arrive early for the exams.
13. Do not be late for exams or you will not have enough time.
14. Always revise your answers to make sure you did the correct thing.
15. Try to finish always within the given time so that you have time to go over your answers again.

Make sure that you do your best in order to pass, that you may avoid falling into suicidal thoughts or commit suicide. Even if you fail after much preparation, it is not the end of the world. However, next time prepare yourself adequately.

CHAPTER XXIV

SICKNESS

To become ill is a serious problem. It throws you off board. It disrupts practically everything. If you were concentrating in doing something, you will witness all your activities come to a stand still.

Illness will also make you become depressed, especially if the illness is a serious one or the one that can not be treated. Many people do not only become depressed, but also commit suicide. I still remember of one guy, years ago, who committed suicide by shooting himself because he was impotent.

SOLUTIONS

Do not commit suicide because of your illness, but seek appropriate medical treatments. Even if the illness is very serious and untreatable, do not commit suicide. Fight on. Anything is possible. You may have your miracle even if the type of illness is totally untreatable. We have witnessed on many occasions, some patients getting well miraculously from dreaded diseases. You too could be in this number. Do not worry. You will get well again, fight on.

TURN TO HIGH POWER

If you have tried everything and nothing has worked for you, turn to God Almighty who is the conqueror of everything. We have witnessed the powers of prayer. Diseases that can not be treated are normally healed through prayers. Do not doubt this, it works. If it works for others, it will work for you too, but do not look at suicide as the solution. It is not a solution at all, but trouble and a complete disaster.

CHAPTER XXV

YOUR PARENTS

Your parents are great people. They always love you despite the mistakes you might make. They will always make sure that you have the best in life. When you succeed in life, it is always their joy, and they will always feel proud of you.

Your parents looked after you when you arrived in this world. They sent you to schools so that you may have knowledge and a better life. Even if they had nothing, yet they made sure that you receive your education even if hunger was wrecking the family. You were their priority to everything in life.

YOUR BEHAVIOUR

Even though they are very good to you and have always provided you with almost everything, yet if you misbehave, it will totally upset them. This may also lead to withdrawals of some of your privileges and some other requirements. This kind of step is taken to drive some senses into your head they are by no means a sign of hatred. And you should know this. And if you know that you are wrong just admit it to them openly and ask for forgiveness. Sure enough, they will forgive you and continue to love you as ever because you are their child. Do not let anything they do and they say, disturb and frustrate you to the point of having suicidal thoughts, or trying to commit suicide. No, your parents sincerely love you even if they sometimes get annoyed with you. You will realize this when you will be married and have children, then you will be able to see clearly the love of your parents for you and you will appreciate everything they have done for you.

If you have any issue with your parents, go and tell them openly, however avoid at all costs quarrelling. It is not the right thing to do. Love them just like they love you, and still love you. You must also that your parents are with you to the end. Do not therefore disappoint them by talking of committing suicide, you will break their hearts and you may make them even die prematurely because of worrying to lose you. Be kind and fair, and do not pay, good with evil. Never think of and never talk of committing suicide.